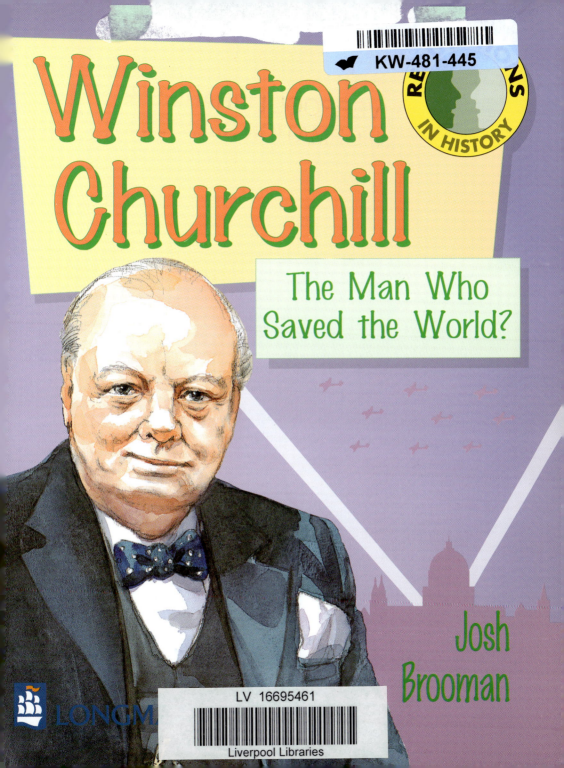

Winston Churchill

The Man Who Saved the World?

REPUTATIONS IN HISTORY

Josh Brooman

LONGM

To the reader

Many of us have a reputation for something. Do you? Do people say, for example, that you are good at sport, or that you are a brilliant dancer? Perhaps they admire your computer skills, or even your ability to tell jokes?

Some of us have a good reputation but some do not. It's easy, for example, to get a reputation for always being late, or for talking too much, or for being mean.

Usually we deserve our reputation, but sometimes it can be unfair. People might say you have no dress sense simply because they are jealous of the way you look. They might call you a show-off just because they dislike you for being popular.

History is a little like this. There are thousands of men and women in history who have reputations both good and bad. But do they deserve them? Have they been judged fairly?

That is what this book is about. It asks you to think about the reputation of one of Britain's most famous Prime Ministers, Winston Churchill, who led the country during the Second World War.

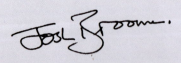

2

Contents

Introduction

Some years ago, I helped to make a video about the Second World War. The government wanted schoolchildren to celebrate the 50th anniversary of the end of the Second World War, so it sent a teaching pack about the war to every school in the country. The video was in the pack.

As soon as it appeared, there was a great fuss in the newspapers. The *Sun* said that it was 'nonsense'. The *Daily Telegraph* called it a 'video of grotesque errors'. The *Daily Mail* declared, 'It is an insult.'

The problem, said the *Daily Mail*, was that the video 'betrayed Winston Churchill'. 'The man who led the nation to victory features for only 14 seconds' in the 24-minute video. 'This is a gross insult to the memory of my grandfather,' wrote Churchill's granddaughter in the *Sun*. 'He was the man who saved the free world.'

Were they right? Exactly how much time and space should a video about the Second World War give to Winston Churchill? And was he the man who saved the free world? It is for you to decide after reading this book.

This photograph of Winston Churchill was taken in the Cabinet Room at 10 Downing Street in September 1940, four months after he became Prime Minister.

Chapter 1

Churchill before the War

When the Second World War began, Winston Churchill was nearly 65 years old. Behind him was a long and varied career. Anyone looking back at it could see an amazing mixture of successes and failures.

A Conservative, then a Liberal

Churchill's career began in 1901 when he became a Member of Parliament. He belonged to the Conservative Party, but soon he began to disagree with its ideas. After only three years he decided to leave the Party. He got up from his seat in the House of Commons and crossed over to the benches where Liberal MPs sat.

Churchill's jobs in the government

Soon after joining the Liberal Party, Churchill was given a job in the government, looking after the colonies in the British Empire. This was the first in a long line of government posts which he held during the next 25 years. In each one he did important work and made some important changes.

As President of the Board of Trade (1908–10) he set up labour exchanges to help people who were out of work to find jobs. As Home Secretary (1910–11) he improved conditions in prisons by ending solitary confinement, and he reduced the number of people in prisons. As First Lord of the Admiralty (1911–15) he modernised the Royal Navy with new battleships and a naval air service. The Navy was, therefore, ready for war when the First World War began in 1914. As Minister for Munitions (1916–18) during the war, he began the large-scale production of a new weapon, the tank. It was to play a major part in winning the war. And as secretary for war and air (1918–20), he brought millions of soldiers home at the end of the war and returned them to civilian life.

Back to the Conservative Party

In 1922 Churchill was beaten in an election, so he had to leave Parliament and his government job. He was soon back. He did this by leaving the Liberal Party in 1924 and then standing as an independent candidate in a by-election. He won, and, soon after returning to Parliament, was given one of the top three jobs in government. He became Chancellor of the Exchequer, in charge of the nation's finances. Shortly after, he rejoined the Conservative Party.

Mistakes: Tonypandy (1910) ...

In all but one of these jobs, Churchill made mistakes which harmed his reputation. As Home Secretary (1908–11) he sent 300 policemen to South Wales when miners rioted during a strike at Tonypandy. There was ugly fighting as the police used their truncheons against the miners. As a result, he gained a reputation as an enemy of working people.

... Gallipoli (1915) ...

His biggest failure came in 1915, during the First World War. As First Lord of the Admiralty, he wanted to use the Navy to fight Turkey, one of Britain's enemies. In 1915 he planned an attack on a part of Turkey called Gallipoli. The attack failed and 200,000 soldiers were killed or wounded. Churchill was blamed for this disaster and was moved to a less important job in the government.

... Russia (1918–19) ...

Also unsuccessful was a war plan which he made while he was secretary for war and air. Communists had taken over the government in Russia in 1917. Churchill hated Communism, and sent British forces to Russia to help enemies of the Communists. They took over a few towns but never fought the Communists in battle. They were brought back to Britain a year later after achieving nothing.

... The gold standard and the General Strike (1926)

As Chancellor (1924–29), Churchill put the British pound back on the 'gold standard'. This meant giving the pound a fixed value against other currencies. But the value he chose was too high, and businesses found it hard to sell their goods to other countries.

This weakened an already weak economy and, in 1926, millions of workers came out on a General Strike. Churchill strongly opposed the strike and did all he could to weaken the strikers by starting up an emergency newspaper called the *British Gazette*. This reminded many people of his actions against the strikers in South Wales in 1910, so it added to his reputation as an enemy of ordinary working people.

The wilderness years

In 1929 there was a general election. Although Churchill won his own seat, many other Conservatives lost theirs to the Labour Party. As a result, Labour took power and so Churchill was out of the government. He spent the next ten years as an ordinary MP, making speeches and writing for the newspapers, but holding no power. He called these his 'wilderness years'.

He opposes freedom for India

During those ten years, Churchill did all he could to oppose the government on two issues. The first was to do with India, which was part of the British Empire. When the government made plans to give India more freedom, Churchill tried to prevent it. Few people outside the Commons agreed with him. Public opinion was in favour of loosening Britain's ties with India. Churchill's campaign to stop this made him seem out of touch with ordinary people's views.

He opposes German rearmament

The second issue was to do with Germany. Many Germans hated the way they had been treated at the end of the First World War, and supported a leader who promised to rebuild Germany's power – Adolf Hitler. He became the leader of Germany in 1933 and immediately began to build up the German armed forces. Even though this was forbidden by international law, the British government did not try to stop him.

Churchill angrily opposed this. He said that Britain should also build its armed forces to stop Hitler from rearming Germany. But the government ignored him. Many people agreed that Germany had been badly treated, and did not think that Hitler was entirely wrong. Moreover, few people wanted to risk another war so soon after the First World War had ended. And even if they were prepared to risk war, the government simply did not have the money to build up a big army in peacetime.

He opposes the policy of appeasement

For all these reasons, the government followed a policy of appeasement towards Hitler. This meant agreeing to some of his demands as a way of stopping him from going to war to get what he wanted.

The most famous episode in the policy of appeasement took place in 1938 when the British Prime Minister, Neville Chamberlain, flew to Munich in Germany for a conference with Hitler. He went there because Hitler was threatening to take over a part of Czechoslovakia where many German-speaking people lived. This could have led to a war between Germany and Czechoslovakia's allies, France and Britain. Chamberlain wanted to settle the problem peacefully. Churchill urged him to make war on Germany.

At the Munich Conference, Chamberlain agreed that Germany could have the part of Czechoslovakia which Hitler wanted. In return, Hitler promised that he would not take any more land from other countries in future. Chamberlain returned to Britain saying that there would be 'peace in our time'. Churchill called it 'a total disaster'.

Looking back, we can now see that Churchill was right and Chamberlain was wrong, for Hitler soon broke his promise. Only six months later, he sent the German army to take over the rest of Czechoslovakia. This is shown on page 15.

Churchill back in the government

Chamberlain still hoped that Hitler could be stopped by appeasing him. But when German forces invaded Poland in September 1939, he admitted that appeasement had failed, and declared war on Germany. To direct the war, he invited a group of senior politicians to form a War Cabinet. One of them was Winston Churchill – he was given his old job as First Lord of the Admiralty, in charge of the Royal Navy.

No. 1,281

TWOPENCE

Sunday Pictorial

THE QUEEN
Page 7

Hitler Plans New 'Peace' Trap

ANOTHER HITLER "PEACE" TRAP IS EXPECTED SOON. THIS ONE WILL BE BAITED MORE CUNNINGLY.

IT WILL BE A REAL DIPLOMATIC OFFENSIVE. THE REICHSTAG HAS BEEN SUMMONED TO MEET THIS WEEK TO HEAR A STATEMENT BY THE NAZI GOVERNMENT, AND THE NEW CAMPAIGN IS LIKELY TO OPEN THEN.

First move in the Nazi manœuvre was the summoning of Count Ciano, Italian Foreign Minister, to Berlin. He will arrive to-day.

The visit is stated to be connected with the German-Soviet pact's reference to the joint efforts of the two signatories that may be undertaken, if necessary, in accord with "other friendly Powers" to get a lightning peace.

The peace trick contained in the pact with Stalin was so blatant that Hitler knew it would leave Britain and France cold. But it was an attempt to shift the war guilt on to the shoulders of the Allies, to bamboozle the German people and to impress neutrals. The most potent neutral is not deceived—Roosevelt.

And yesterday Nazi diplomacy received a severe rebuff. The Turkish Embassy in London was officially informed that a Turkish military mission is on its way to London.

This supported reports that Britain and Turkey will shortly sign a mutual assistance pact, a diplomatic victory for Britain which will radically influence the vital Eastern Mediterranean situation.

More surprising news came from Moscow last night. Stalin is behaving mysteriously towards Turkey, though Rome radio reported that Turkey and Russia have reached an agreement to close the Dardanelles, to all belligerents.

Continued on Back Page

THIS IS THE MAN He Fears!

"Churchill Will Be Our Next Premier"—See Page 9

This newspaper appeared several weeks after Churchill joined the War Cabinet. It shows that many people, right from the start of the war, saw Churchill as the man to beat Hitler.

Task: was Churchill a good choice for the War Cabinet in 1939?

1 Look back at pages 6–11 and find 12 events in Churchill's career before 1939. On a table like the one below, put in column 1 any event which you think was a success. Put any event which you think was a failure in column 2. In column 3 explain why you think each event was a success or a failure.

Winston Churchill's career before the Second World War		
Success	Failure	Explanation

2 A public opinion poll in 1939 found that 50 per cent of the public thought that Churchill should be in the War Cabinet, and 25 per cent thought that he should not. Use your completed table to write a one-minute conversation in which two members of the public, Frank Lee and May Isay, are arguing about whether Churchill should be in the War Cabinet. The conversation could begin like this:

Frank Churchill's a good man to have in the War Cabinet. He's had a lot of experience in government. In the last war he was First Lord of the Admiralty …

May (Interrupts) Yes, and just look what a mess he made of that. At Gallipoli …

Chapter 2

Churchill becomes Prime Minister

Evacuation, gas masks and air-raid precautions

Britain went to war with Germany on 3rd September 1939. Over the next few weeks, 1.5 million women and children were evacuated from their homes. As a defence against poison gas, 38 million gas masks were given out to the whole population. Air-raid shelters were built, anti-aircraft guns were set up around the cities, and a 'blackout' banned the use of lights in the open at night.

A phoney war

And yet the British armed forces did not go to war. It was, in reality, very difficult for Britain and France to help Poland fight their enemies. Poland was 1,000 kilometres away, and Britain's forces were small. So, when German and Soviet armies marched into Poland in September 1939, the British and French did nothing to stop them. People said that Britain was in a 'phoney war' – at war with Germany but not fighting.

Neville Chamberlain, the Prime Minister, was not unhappy with this. He wanted to build up Britain's forces before attacking Germany. Meanwhile, the Navy would stop food, oil and essential goods from reaching Germany. Germany would then be on the point of collapse when Britain was ready to invade in about three years' time.

The two sides and their leaders at the start of the Second World War

Britain's side: Britain and France promised to defend Poland if Germany attacked Poland.

Neville Chamberlain	Édouard Daladier	Ignacy Moscicki

Britain

Poland

Soviet Union

Germany

2 3

1

France

Italy

Adolf Hitler	Benito Mussolini	Josef Stalin

Germany's side: Hitler had an agreement with Mussolini that they would help each other in any war. Hitler also had an agreement with Stalin that they would not fight each other over Poland. In addition, they secretly agreed to divide Poland between them after Germany had conquered it.

Key: Land taken by Germany in 1938–39
1 Austria
2 Sudetenland
3 Bohemia and Moravia

15

Churchill's Norway plan

Churchill supported Chamberlain in this, but really he wanted immediate action. He bombarded Chamberlain with ideas for using the Royal Navy against Germany. Eventually, Chamberlain agreed to a plan to send British forces to Norway.

Look at the map on the next page. You will see two reasons why Churchill wanted to send forces to Norway. The first was to help Finland fight the Soviet Army, which attacked it in November 1939. The second was to stop Germany from making weapons. To make weapons, German factories needed iron ore. Most of this came down the Baltic Sea from Sweden. In the winter, when the Baltic was frozen, trains took the ore to Narvik, in Norway, where it was loaded on to ships for Germany. If the British could stop these ships, Germany would not be able to make weapons.

The plan is changed

By March 1940, 100,000 soldiers had gathered to invade Norway. Then Churchill's plan fell apart, for Finland made peace with the Soviet Union. This took away the main reason for the invasion. The invasion force had to be broken up.

Churchill did not give up all his hopes for Norway, and drew up a new plan. British warships would put explosive mines in the sea along the coast of Norway. Any ship taking iron ore to Germany would be blown up and sunk if it touched a mine.

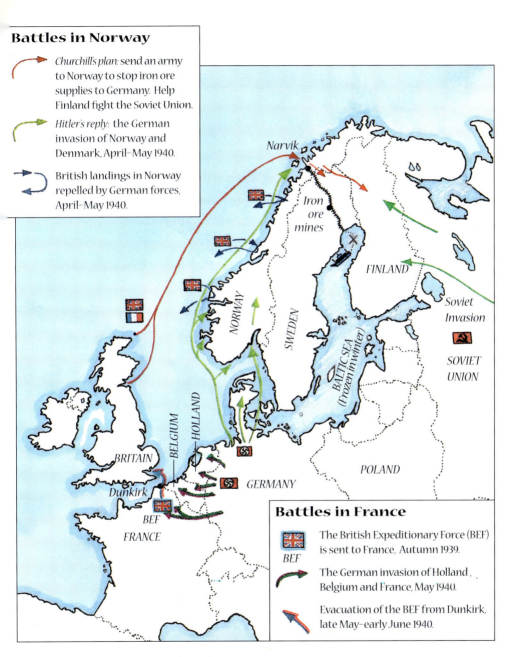

Battles in Norway

Churchill's plan: send an army to Norway to stop iron ore supplies to Germany. Help Finland fight the Soviet Union.

Hitler's reply: the German invasion of Norway and Denmark, April–May 1940.

British landings in Norway repelled by German forces, April–May 1940.

Narvik

Iron ore mines

FINLAND

Soviet Invasion

SOVIET UNION

NORWAY

SWEDEN

BALTIC SEA (Frozen in winter)

POLAND

BELGIUM

HOLLAND

BRITAIN

Dunkirk

BEF

FRANCE

GERMANY

Battles in France

The British Expeditionary Force (BEF) is sent to France, Autumn 1939.

BEF

The German invasion of Holland, Belgium and France, May 1940.

Evacuation of the BEF from Dunkirk, late May–early June 1940.

Britain's first battles with Germany, May–June 1940.

The plan fails

British ships started dropping the mines into the sea on 8th April. But Hitler had been expecting such a move. For months he had been planning his own invasion of Norway. Now he put it into action. On the same day as the British were laying their mines, German forces seized every important port along the Norwegian coast.

Total confusion followed. Britain's invasion force was quickly reassembled. But now it had to do something for which it was not equipped – attack a coast defended by Germans. When they came ashore, they were hammered by German planes and had to withdraw.

This was a disaster for the War Cabinet. After seven months without fighting, British forces had been defeated in their first action against the enemy. The House of Commons met on 7th May to discuss why things had gone so badly wrong. Although the plan to invade Norway had been Churchill's, it was Chamberlain who many MPs now blamed. They blamed him for appeasing Hitler in 1938, and they blamed him for taking so little action when the war began in 1939.

Conservatives turn against Chamberlain

This should not have been a problem for Chamberlain. He was the leader of the Conservatives, and more MPs belonged to the Conservative Party than any other. In normal times, they would have voted loyally in support of their leader. But these were not normal times. 101 Conservative MPs believed that a stronger war leader was needed. They voted against him, along with the MPs of the other parties.

If a Prime Minister loses the support of so many MPs, he or she has to resign. This is what Chamberlain now prepared to do. But who should take his place? It would have to be somebody already in the War Cabinet, and there were only two possible men for the job. One was Lord Halifax, who most Conservatives wanted. The other was Winston Churchill, who was very popular and had strong public support.

Churchill or Halifax?

Chamberlain called the two men to a meeting at 10 Downing Street and asked Churchill whether he thought Halifax should be Prime Minister. If Churchill had said yes, the job would almost certainly have gone to Halifax. But he did not answer the question. He went to the window and looked out, in silence, for a full two minutes.

Churchill's silence made Halifax realise that Churchill would not work with him if he became Prime Minister. Yet Churchill was so popular that Halifax could not afford to do without him. Halifax broke the silence by telling Chamberlain that it would not be possible for him to become Prime Minister. The next day, Chamberlain resigned and Winston Churchill became Prime Minister in his place.

Task: was it a surprise that Churchill became Prime Minister?

It is 10th May 1940. Churchill has just become Prime Minister. Frank Lee and May Isay are arguing about the news – again. As before, Frank is for Churchill and May is against. Write a second conversation between them by completing the starters below, wherever you see three dots. All the information you need is on the page numbers shown in *italics*.

Frank   Chamberlain was useless. He did nothing to help Poland last year.

May   What could he do? Poland … (*page 14*)

Frank   So what does he get us all doing instead? Evacuation … (*page 14*)

May   Not just that. His idea was to build up our forces before attacking Germany … (*page 14*)

Frank   Yes, but that would have taken years. Churchill had the right idea with his idea of invading Norway … (*page 16*)

May   But the Norway plan failed.

Frank   That wasn't Churchill's fault. It failed because … (*page 16*)

May   Even if it wasn't his fault, why should Chamberlain be blamed when it wasn't his idea?

Frank   Well, Norway wasn't his first mistake, was it? He was wrong from the start with his policy of appeasement … (*pages 10–11*)

Chapter 3

Churchill, Dunkirk and the Battle of Britain

Churchill became Prime Minister on 10th May 1940. He faced a terrible crisis immediately. On that day, 2.5 million German soldiers attacked Holland and Belgium without warning. Three days later they attacked France, Britain's main ally.

A change of aim: 'Victory, however long and hard ...'

Facing the Germans was a large French army and a much smaller British army – the British Expeditionary Force (BEF). Churchill had no doubt about what the BEF should do. On 13th May he made a speech to Parliament, telling MPs what he planned to do as Prime Minister. He said:

> I have nothing to offer but blood, toil, tears and sweat ... You ask, what is our policy? I will say, it is to wage war, by sea, land and air ... You ask, what is our aim? I can answer in one word. Victory ... however long and hard the road may be.

Although Churchill was offering them 'blood, toil, tears and sweat', British people were thrilled and inspired by his speech. He was offering the exact opposite of Neville Chamberlain's policy. Instead of blockading Germany in a 'phoney war', Britain would now fight Germany head on – and win.

The BEF in France

There was, in fact, little that the BEF could do. In just one week, the German forces smashed their way through northern France and took control of a corridor of land stretching all the way to the Channel coast. The BEF was on one side of the corridor, the French on the other. Churchill ordered the BEF to attack this corridor and to link up with the French. But they had too few planes and big guns to drive the Germans back. Their attack ground to a halt.

Churchill now realised that the BEF would never be able to join up with the French. He ordered the army to return to Britain. This was an almost impossible order, for it meant bringing nearly half a million men, chased by the German forces, across the Channel. Churchill did not expect more than a tenth of them to return, and he warned the British public to expect terrible news.

Evacuation from Dunkirk

In fact, the order succeeded beyond his best hopes. When the BEF reached the Channel coast at Dunkirk, the Royal Navy organised a huge rescue operation. Several hundred warships went to the coast in 'Operation Dynamo'. They were helped by volunteers in hundreds of small boats such as trawlers. Between 26th May and 4th June, 865 boats rescued 215,587 British soldiers and 127,031 French soldiers from the beaches at Dunkirk.

This was a wonderful achievement, but it was not a victory. Although 330,000 men had been saved, they had left behind nearly all their guns and tanks. The Navy had lost six warships and the Royal Air Force (RAF) had lost nearly 500 planes.

Churchill rejects peace ...

Hitler thought that the British would not want to continue the war after this, so he offered to make peace with Britain. Churchill refused even to think about it. He said that Britain would go on fighting until Germany surrendered, and took a series of emergency measures to defend the country.

... and prepares Britain's defences

The priority was to make more planes for the RAF. Until now, as you have read, the government's policy was to build up its weapons slowly and carefully. Now, workers in the aircraft factories worked ten hours a day for seven days a week. To provide them with metal, garden railings all over the country were cut down. Housewives were asked to give up their aluminium pans.

This was only one of the ways in which ordinary people were asked to help in the war effort. Men were urged to join a force which Churchill named the Home Guard. These volunteers did what they could to prepare for invasion. They set up road blocks. They took down road signs to confuse

German drivers. And they trained to fight the Germans, even though many did not have rifles. Women too were asked to do war work. They were urged to join the armed forces in non-combat roles, or to work in factories or on farms.

As a result, millions of ordinary men and women soon came to feel that they were involved in a 'people's war' to save their country from invasion. Posters like the one opposite strengthened this feeling of unity.

The Battle of Britain

The first stage of the invasion began in mid-July 1940. It was carried out by the German Air Force. Its orders were to destroy Britain's Royal Air Force so that the ships bringing German forces across the Channel would be safe from air attack. Throughout the summer of 1940 German and British fighter pilots fought each other in the skies above southern England. Churchill called it 'The Battle of Britain'.

By the end of the summer the RAF was close to defeat. It did not have enough pilots and its airfields were badly damaged. Then, on 7th September, came an amazing turnaround. The Germans stopped attacking the RAF airfields and started dropping bombs on London instead. They did this in revenge for British bombing raids on Berlin. This gave the RAF a chance to recover its strength and reorganise its forces.

"LET US GO FORWARD TOGETHER"

This poster came out in May 1940, when Churchill became Prime Minister. The words are from the speech in which he said 'I have nothing to offer but blood, toil, tears and sweat' (see page 21). He ended by saying, 'I feel entitled to claim the aid of all, and I say "Come then, let us go forward together with our united strength."'

A week later, the RAF shot down 60 German aircraft on a bombing raid over London. From then on, the Germans stopped daytime bombing and went over to night-time bombing. This meant that the RAF kept control of the air space over Britain, and could attack any invasion force. Hitler had to cancel his invasion plan.

Public opinion

Throughout the summer of 1940 Britain was close to defeat. Yet public opinion polls showed that Churchill was more popular than any Prime Minister before him. Even though defeat was staring them in the face, 89 per cent of the public said they thought he was a good leader.

There were many reasons why people felt like this. One was a belief that Churchill was well suited to lead the country in wartime. The interviewers who carried out opinion polls heard many comments that 'he is for war and not peace', 'he's hard', 'he's a match for Hitler', or 'he's the right man in the right place'. People thought this because of Churchill's past record in the First World War, and because he had spoken out against German rearmament in the 1930s (see page 10).

A second reason for Churchill's popularity was the image created by the news media – newspapers, cinema newsreels, and radio. It was a very distinctive image. Photographs and newsreels nearly always showed him smoking a fat cigar. He wore unusual clothes, and was the only Prime Minister ever to wear military uniform while in office. And people were often surprised to see him with two fingers in the air, giving what he called his Victory sign.

Many people also saw Churchill in person. He often left his government offices to visit workers in factories, or to show sympathy for people whose homes had been damaged by bombs. The photograph on the next page shows the welcome he was given when he toured Swansea on 12th April 1941.

Speeches

More even than his appearance, Churchill's voice created an image that people recognised and liked. Churchill made many speeches in Parliament during the war. When he repeated some of these speeches on the radio, around 70 per cent of the population listened to them. Probably the most famous was the speech he made on 4th June 1940, after the BEF had returned from Dunkirk. In it, he said:

> We shall defend our island, whatever the cost may be. We shall fight on the beaches, we shall fight on the landing grounds, we shall fight in the fields and in the streets, we shall fight in the hills; we shall never surrender ...

This photograph was taken on 12th April 1941 in Swansea, in South Wales. It shows Winston Churchill raising a laugh while on his way to inspect bomb damage in the city docks. He said while he was there, 'There is a good spirit in the town. The people are standing up to the bombing well.'

Task: why was Churchill so popular in 1940?

Look at the photograph opposite. Imagine that Churchill has gone by and that the girl in the front is talking with her mother. Part of their conversation is shown below. Complete it by adding information taken from the pages shown in *italics*.

Mum	Remember what you've seen. When you're older you'll be able to tell your grandchildren you saw Winston Churchill this close.
Girl	Why does everybody think he's so good? Why did everybody cheer when he went past?
Mum	Lots of reasons. As soon as he became Prime Minister, he changed the way we were fighting the war. He made a famous speech. He said that …(*page 21*)
Girl	But we haven't had a victory yet, have we?
Mum	That's true. Our army in France … (*pages 22–23*)
Girl	So why did everybody cheer him just then?
Mum	Well, last summer, in 1940, the Germans were getting ready to invade us. Churchill got everybody to join in to help stop it … (*pages 23–24*)
Girl	And is that why the Germans didn't invade us?
Mum	Not just that. The main reason was that the RAF won the Battle of Britain … (*pages 24 and 26*)

Chapter 4

Churchill's World War

When Churchill took power, the war was being fought in Europe. Soon it spread to all parts of the globe. For the next five years, Churchill led Britain in a world war.

Britain's war in the Mediterranean

The war spread first into the Mediterranean region. It did so because Mussolini, the leader of Italy, wanted to control the Mediterranean Sea. Churchill could not allow this, for British ships used the Mediterranean to trade with Britain's colonies in the Far East. To protect this shipping route, the Royal Navy had bases in Gibraltar and Malta. A British army in Egypt protected the Suez Canal.

The Mediterranean war began badly for Italy. In September 1940, 300,000 Italian soldiers attacked the British army in Egypt. Although outnumbered ten to one, the British halted them and advanced into Libya. A month later, the Italians invaded Greece. Again their attack failed, and the Greeks threw them out of their country.

These defeats worried Hitler. He did not want Britain to get any stronger in the Mediterranean, so he decided to help Mussolini. He sent armies to Greece and Yugoslavia, and he sent General Rommel's Afrika Korps to North Africa.

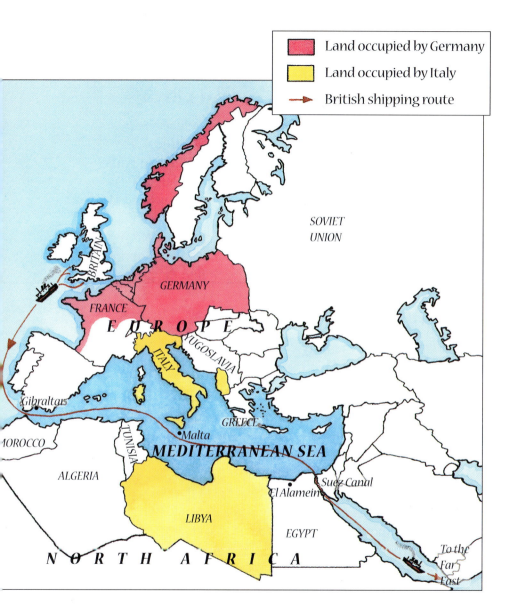

This map shows the places around the Mediterranean where British forces fought in the Second World War.

British defeats in Greece and Libya

In reply, Churchill decided to help the Greeks defend their country. He sent 62,000 British soldiers from North Africa to Greece. It was a disaster. The Germans defeated them in battle and forced them to leave Greece within days. Although 50,000 soldiers escaped, they left behind nearly all their tanks and guns. A second disaster quickly followed. While Churchill was sending soldiers to Greece, Rommel's soldiers were arriving in North Africa. With so many British soldiers away in Greece, Rommel drove the British army out of Libya and back into Egypt.

Churchill looks for allies

Britain was by now the only country still fighting Germany. Its only ally, France, had surrendered in June 1940. So Churchill looked for new allies.

The country which he most wanted as an ally was the United States of America. He tried to persuade its President, Franklin Roosevelt, to join the war. Many Americans did want to help, for they admired the way Britain was standing up to Germany. The poster opposite reflects that view. But wanting to help was not the same as wanting to fight. Opinion polls showed that 19 out of 20 Americans wanted to keep out of the war. All Roosevelt could do was give Britain help in the form of weapons.

Even then, help was very limited. In mid-1940, Roosevelt gave Britain 50 warships that the USA did not need.

This poster was painted by an American artist in 1940. It shows Churchill as a British bulldog defending Britain – 'holding the line' – against Germany.

In return, Churchill had to give the USA the right to use British bases around the world for 99 years. But when the ships arrived in Britain, they were in such bad condition that only nine could be used. Then, in 1941, Roosevelt started a 'lend-lease' plan to lend Britain war materials. Again there was less material than was needed, and again there were strings attached.

It was not until the end of 1941 that the USA finally joined the war, and then it was not of Churchill's doing. Roosevelt declared war on Japan when it attacked Pearl Harbor, a US navy base in the Pacific Ocean. As Japan was an ally of Germany, the USA also went to war with Germany. Britain at last had the USA as its ally.

The Soviet Union

Churchill gained another valuable ally in mid-1941 when German forces invaded the Soviet Union. As you have read (page 8) Churchill hated the Communist government in the Soviet Union, and he had sent armies to try to crush it back in 1919. Now he forgot his dislike of Communism. He promised the Soviet leader, Stalin, that Britain would help the Soviet people fight the German invaders.

Singapore

This was of no immediate help, for Britain soon suffered a terrible defeat. When Japan entered the war in 1941, one of its aims was to capture Britain's colonies in the Far East in order

The Soviet Union, the United States of America and Britain became allies in 1941, and they remained allies for the rest of the war. Their leaders, Stalin, Roosevelt, and Churchill were known as 'the Big Three'. They are shown here at a meeting in Yalta, in the Soviet Union, in 1945.

to take their resources, such as oil. To protect those colonies, Britain had a powerful military base at Singapore. But it was not as powerful as it should have been. For years, the government had been cutting costs, and Singapore's guns and aircraft were out of date. Then, after the war began, so many British soldiers were sent to the Mediterranean that Singapore did not have enough men or weapons to defend itself.

When Japan declared war at the end of 1941, Churchill tried desperately to strengthen Singapore. At his suggestion, the Navy sent two of its most powerful warships to the Far East, *Prince of Wales* and *Repulse*. But Japanese aircraft caught the ships at sea and sank them in deep water.

Soon after, Japanese forces attacked Singapore itself. Churchill gave orders that Singapore 'must be defended to the death', and added 'commanders are expected to die at their posts'. But before the commanders had a chance to die at their posts, they ran so short of water, petrol and ammunition that it became impossible to fight. They surrendered on 15th February 1942. 150,000 British Empire troops were taken prisoner. It was Britain's worst-ever military disaster.

From bad to worse in North Africa

The situation was no better in North Africa. After Rommel's victory in 1941, Churchill had sacked the Commander of the British forces there. The man who replaced him did better for a while. He counter-attacked and forced Rommel to retreat. Hitler, though, was determined that Rommel must not be beaten, and sent him more men and equipment. In May 1942 Rommel struck again. After a month's fighting, he broke the British defences at Gazala and took 30,000 prisoners.

This made Churchill's position very difficult. In Parliament, some MPs criticised him. For the first time in the war, ordinary people started to question his leadership. Churchill knew that he must produce a victory to silence his critics.

Bomber offensive

Since 1940 the British and German airforces had been dropping bombs on each other's ports and factories, trying to destroy each other's trade and industry. They failed. Their bombs did not always hit the target. When they did, the damage was not always bad. So, in 1942, Churchill agreed to a new kind of bombing – 'area bombing'. This meant dropping bombs on whole cities, not just ports and factories. The aim was to terrify the Germans so badly that they would lose the will to fight.

At first, it seemed that this 'bomber offensive' could not fail. Using hundreds, sometimes thousands of planes for a single raid, RAF Bomber Command caused damage on a scale never seen before in the history of the world. By 1945 they had killed over 800,000 people and made 7.5 million homeless in 131 cities. Yet the Germans did not lose their will to fight. Most people did not panic or despair. They continued to live and work in the ruins of their cities. So the bomber offensive did not provide the rapid victory that Churchill needed.

A 'second front', or Operation Torch?

It wasn't only the British who wanted results from Churchill in 1942. His new allies also wanted some quick victories. The Soviet Union was close to defeat and Stalin wanted the British and American armies to attack the Germans in France. This would create a 'second front' in the war, and the Germans would have to divide their forces to defend it. That would take pressure off the Soviet Union.

Roosevelt also wanted to invade France. With elections for the Presidency coming up, he wanted to show American voters that the war was going well. A victory over the German forces in France would be a good starting point.

Churchill ruled out an invasion of France in 1942. He said that it would take at least a year to gather an invasion force of sufficient strength. Instead he persuaded Roosevelt that the British and Americans should invade northwest Africa in an operation code-named Torch. An American general, Eisenhower, was put in command.

The Battle of El Alamein

But a British–American invasion, led by an American, would not give Churchill the victory he needed. In August 1942 he flew to Egypt where the British army was in retreat from the Germans. He sacked the army commander and put General Sir Bernard Montgomery in command of the eighth army.

Montgomery steadily built up his forces until the 8th Army had 230,000 soldiers against Rommel's 80,000; 1,000 tanks to Rommel's 500; 1,500 aircraft to Rommel's 350. Then, on 23th October, he launched his attack at El Alamein. Although outnumbered, Rommel's forces fought with great skill. It was not until 4th November that British tanks broke though his lines, captured 20,000 prisoners, and started to chase the rest of his forces into Libya. Churchill at last had a victory.

The Torch landings

The Battle of El Alamein was the first and last great victory that the British army won alone. For the rest of the war, British forces fought alongside their allies. They soon won an important victory. Four days after the Battle of El Alamein ended, the Allied forces began Operation Torch – the invasion of North Africa. They landed in Morocco and Algeria, and advanced eastwards. From the other direction, Montgomery was chasing Rommel as he retreated from El Alamein. Slowly, they drove Rommel's forces back into Tunisia. They surrendered in May 1943.

The invasion of Italy

Now that the Allies controlled North Africa, they could

attack Italy. Italy by now was very weak. Churchill called it 'the soft underbelly' of Europe. In July 1943, half a million Allied soldiers landed on Sicily. But far from being 'soft', Italy proved hard to defeat, for Hitler sent huge numbers of German soldiers to Italy to fight the Allies. It took the Allies more than a year to fight their way up through Italy. The invasion of Italy therefore seemed like a mistake. But one thing could be said in its favour. It tied down many German soldiers needed to defend Germany against an even greater Allied invasion – Operation Overlord in 1944.

Operation Overlord

Operation Overlord began on 6th June 1944 – code-named D-Day. 156,000 US, British and Canadian troops, supported by 8,000 ships and 13,000 aircraft, landed in Normandy in Northern France. After heavy fighting in which 10,000 Allied soldiers died, they forced the Germans to retreat and made their way inland. They slowly wore down the German defences with massive air and land attacks. At the end of July they finally broke the German lines and swept through Northern France.

Churchill the world statesman

Churchill was closely involved in all these actions. From 1940 to 1945 he made frequent journeys overseas for meetings with the Allied leaders. At these meetings, they made decisions about how to fight the war and about what they should do when it was over.

This painting, by British artist Terence Cuneo, shows British soldiers landing on a beach in Normandy at the start of Operation Overlord in June 1944.

Churchill's most important meetings were with Roosevelt and Stalin. Together they were known as 'the Big Three', and they made decisions which had far-reaching effects for the world. They decided, for example, to divide Germany at the end of the war so that it could never fight a war again. They also agreed to set up a 'United Nations' organisation to keep the peace at the end of the war.

The end of the war

Early in 1945 the Allies closed in on Germany – the British and Americans from the west, the Soviets from the east. By May they controlled the whole country. When they entered the capital, Berlin, Hitler committed suicide. Soon after, a new government surrendered to the Allies and the war in Europe came to an end.

The war against Japan went on for another 14 weeks. The Japanese fought with incredible determination to stop the Allies from reaching their country, and many people feared that the war would continue for at least another year. Then, in August 1945, the US Air Force dropped two atomic bombs on the cities of Hiroshima and Nagasaki, destroying both cities and killing at least 150,000 people. The Japanese Emperor immediately surrendered, and the Second World War was over.

Task: how successful was Churchill as a war leader?

1 Turn back to each page number shown in column 1, and read about each event shown in column 2. Decide whether the event was a success or a failure for Britain and, on a copy of the chart, tick either column 3 or 4. (If it was neither a success nor a failure put a question mark in each column.) Then, in column 5, explain whether Churchill was responsible for each success and failure.

Page	Event	Success	Failure	Was Churchill responsible?
30	Egypt, 1940			
32	Greece, 1941			
32	Libya, 1941			
32	Bases for destroyers deal with USA			
34	Lend Lease deal with USA			
34	Alliance with USA			
34	Alliance with Soviet Union			
36	Singapore, 1942			
37	Gazala, 1942			
37–38	Bomber Offensive, 1942–45			
39	El Alamein, 1942			
39	Operation Torch, 1942			
40	Invasion of Italy, 1943			
40	Operation Overlord, 1944			
40–42	'Big Three' meetings, 1941–45			
42	Surrender of Germany, 1945			
42	Surrender of Japan, 1945			

2 Look at your completed chart. What does it tell you about Churchill's success as a war leader?

Chapter 5

The cost of victory

As you have read, Churchill helped to make people feel that they were fighting a 'people's war'. When victory came in 1945, many hoped that it would lead to a 'people's peace' – that everyone would help to rebuild Britain and make it a better place for all. In July 1945 they went to the polls to elect a government to do this.

Churchill out, Labour in

The result was a massive defeat for Churchill: the Labour Party won by a landslide and Clement Attlee, the Labour leader, became Prime Minister. The reason for Churchill's defeat was simple. As war leader, he had spent much of his time on world affairs. He had left others in the War Cabinet, such as Attlee, to deal with home affairs. So, while Churchill was planning how to win the war, they were planning what to do when it ended. In particular, they planned to make Britain into a 'welfare state' with health care and social security for all. Although voters admired Churchill and were grateful for what he had done, they now voted for the party which they thought would give them these things.

A welfare state ...

The Labour government quickly put its plans into effect. Over the next five years, it created a National Health Service, a system of national insurance to help the unemployed, and

The Daily Telegraph
and Morning Post

No. 28,048   LONDON, WEDNESDAY, MAY 9, 1945   Printed in LONDON and MANCHESTER   PRICE 1½d.

LONDON
LATE
EDTN.

NATION'S VE OUTBURST OF JOY: ALL-NIGHT CELEBRATIONS

ROYAL FAMILY FIVE TIMES OUT ON PALACE BALCONY

Mr. CHURCHILL: 'NO GREATER DAY IN OUR HISTORY'

A GREAT NATIONAL OUTBURST OF RELIEF AND THANKSGIVING AT THE END OF NEARLY SIX YEARS OF WAR IN EUROPE WAS EPITOMISED YESTERDAY, VE-DAY, BY TREMENDOUS SCENES OF REJOICING IN

VAST CROWDS HAIL THE KING AT PALACE

MR. CHURCHILL'S V SIGN FROM BALCONY

British family instinct inspired tens of thousands of men and women to go to the London home of their King and Queen on VE-Day yesterday to share with them the joy of peace in Europe.

A vast crowd was assembled outside Buckingham Palace throughout the day and until a late hour a joyous and colourful crowd whose enthusiasm rose to a crescendo of patriotic fervour at the occasional appearances on the balcony of the smiling King and Queen and the Princesses.

When they their Majesties Princess

FROM EARLY MORNING vast crowds, celebrating VE-Day, waited outside Buckingham Palace in hopes of seeing their King and Queen.

Their wish was gratified in the afternoon when their Majesties, accompanied by Princess Elizabeth and Princess Margaret, appeared on the balcony and acknowledged with smiles their tumultuous reception.

On the second of their subsequent appearances on the balcony, they came out with Mr. Churchill, who was greeted with wild expressions of delight. Informality and good-fellowship with the rejoicing people were the message of the King's wave of hand and the happy smiles of the Queen and the Premier.

GERMAN FLEET TO GO TO ALLIED PORTS

ADMIRALTY ORDER

The Admiralty announced yesterday that the following orders have been issued for the surrender of the German Fleet:

All German and German-controlled warships, auxiliaries, merchant ships and other craft at sea are being ordered to report their position in plain language to the nearest Allied wireless telegraphy station, and are being given orders to proceed to such Allied ports as directed. They will remain in these ports until further directions are received.

All warships, auxiliaries, merchant ships and other craft in harbour are being ordered to remain in harbour.

U-boats at sea are being ordered to surface in a black flag or som

GERMANS FIGHT RUSSIANS TO LAST MOMENT

The Germans, whose surrender was due to come into effect this morning at one minute past midnight (11.1 Central European Time last night), were fighting to the last moment against the Red Army.

The routine Soviet communiqué reporting on the day's fighting was issued shortly after 11 o'clock, about

2.40 a.m. SURRENDER SCENE AT ALLIED H.Q.

DRAMATIC 15 MINUTES THAT ENDED WAR

HUMBLED GERMANS

From DOUGLAS WILLIAMS,
Daily Telegraph Special Correspondent
RHEIMS, Tuesday.

The war in Europe is over.

At 2.41 a.m. yesterday, in the war room of Gen. Eisenhower's battle headquarters in this ancient city, two German delegates, Adml. Hans Georg von Friedeburg, C-in-C of the German Navy in succession to Doenitz, and Col.-Gen. Gustav Jodl, Chief of Staff of the Wehrmacht, acting jointly on behalf of Doenitz as head of the Reich, unconditionally surrendered all German land, sea and air forces to the Allied armies in the West, and simultaneously to the Russian armies in the East.

The front page of the Daily Telegraph *shows Winston Churchill on the balcony at Buckingham Palace on VE Day (Victory in Europe Day), 8th May 1945, listening to the cheers of an enormous crowd below. With him were the King and Queen, Princess Margaret and the future Queen Elizabeth II (left), then an 18-year-old officer in the Auxiliary Transport Service.*

a system of benefits for people in need. Millions of ordinary people now had the right to free medical treatment and unemployment pay whenever they needed it. In this respect, the war did lead to a 'people's peace'.

... a bankrupt state ...

But in many other ways it did not. Britain was the only Allied country which had fought from the very start to the end of the war. This left it in very bad shape. Factories, docks, mines, railways and roads were worn out. Many thousands of homes had been destroyed by bombs. The government owed £3 billion to other countries. Britain in 1945 was bankrupt.

The only way of recovering from this was to earn money by selling more to other countries, and by buying less from them. As a result, the British people had to go without many things in the years after the war. Some foods and materials were as short as they had been in the war and some were even shorter. Bread, which had never been rationed during the war, was rationed from 1946 to 1948.

... and a weaker state

Britain was not only poorer after the war than before, but also less powerful. In 1939, Britain had been one of the three most powerful countries in the world, with an Empire of 450 million people living in 56 colonies all over the world. The war loosened Britain's grip on its Empire. As you have read, it lost Singapore and its far eastern colonies to the Japanese in 1941. Although Britain reclaimed its colonies at the end of the war, it was impossible to turn back the clock. Many of the colonies now wanted to be free of any kind of foreign rule, whether British or Japanese.

First to go was India. The new Labour government had wanted to free India from British control for many years, and now it also wanted to cut its spending on the Empire. It ended British rule there in 1947. Most other British colonies were freed from British rule in the 20 years after that.

Churchill in power again

In 1951 the voters went to the polls again. This time the Conservatives won, and Churchill returned as Prime Minister for the next four years. However, his government was not unlike the Labour one which it replaced. He continued to spend money on the welfare state. He launched a programme to build 300,000 new homes. Food rationing continued.

Churchill retired as Prime Minister in 1955, but continued as a Member of Parliament for another ten years. Only in 1964 did he agree to retire fully. It was a very short retirement for, within months of leaving Parliament, he died at the age of 90.

You decide – the man who saved the world?

The year is 2020, the 75th anniversary of the end of the Second World War. As in 1995, the government will send every school in the country a teaching pack to help them celebrate the anniversary. One item in the pack will be a 25-minute video about how Britain and its Allies won the war.

You are a writer and historian, and the government has invited you to help make this video. You can put what you want in it, but the government does not want a repeat of the fuss about Churchill in the video of 1995 (see page 4). You must, therefore, put as much as you can about Churchill into the video.

1   You begin by making a storyboard. This is an outline of the video, and each frame of the storyboard outlines one scene. The first has been done for you as an example.

Scene number	1
Time allowed	30 seconds
Summary	Britain went to war in 1939 when Germany invaded Poland. The first seven months of the war were a 'phoney war'.
Film clips to show	Evacuation, gas masks, air-raid precautions. British armed forces preparing for war.

2   Look at your completed storyboard.
   a   What impression of Churchill does your video create?
   b   Does your video support the idea that Churchill was 'the man who saved the free world'? Explain your answer.